Owen Sheers is a poet, novelist and playwright. Twice winner of the Wales Book of the Year, his books of poetry include *Skirrid Hill*, winner of a Somerset Maugham Award, the verse drama *Pink Mist*, winner of the Hay Festival Poetry Medal, and the Wales Book of the Year. In 2018 he was the recipient of the Wilfred Owen Poetry Award. Owen's theatrical work includes *The Two Worlds of Charlie F.*, winner of the Amnesty International Freedom of Expression Award, *Mametz*, and National Theatre Wales's seventy-two-hour *The Passion*. He lives in Wales with his wife and two daughters.

Further praise for *The Green Hollow*:

'I cannot think of any better term than sacred to describe the sixty quietly shattering minutes of viewing that were *Aberfan: The Green Hollow* . . . [A] masterpiece . . . the kind of film for which the international television industry invented awards . . . The softly spoken glory here was Sheers's language, his largely unrhymed verse, tetrameters, pentameters and variations thereon, the loosest of poetry flowing in line with speech rhythms, often so close to prose as to be almost indistinguishable . . . Fifty years on, Owen Sheers has finally offered the tribute due from a laureate, a post which, on this evidence, he may well one day occupy.' Tom Birchenough (on the BBC adaptation), *Arts Desk*

The Green Hollow

Owen Sheers

FABER & FABER

First published in 2018
by Faber & Faber Limited
Bloomsbury House
74–77 Great Russell Street
London WC1B 3DA

This paperback edition published in 2019

Typeset by Faber & Faber Limited
Printed and bound by CPI Group (UK) Ltd, Croydon, CR0 4YY

As seen on the BBC

BBC logo © BBC 2017
BBC and the BBC logo are trademarks of the British Broadcasting Corporation
and are used under licence

A CIP record for this book
is available from the British Library

ISBN 978-0-571-33908-2

For Aberfan

Contents

PART I

Children

As if all the eyes

Aberfan, South Wales, 21 October 1966.
116 children turn in their beds.
A nine-year-old boy, TOMOS DAVIES, opens his curtains.

TOMOS

The journeys will be starting soon.
You can't see them down here in the street
but once they're up and running
their sound's all through the village –
last thing I hear before going to sleep,
and first thing too just after I wake.
Or when we're playing down the river
or in school on a break.
Rumble they do, and clang.
Metal wheels on metal tracks.
Drams they call them too,
carrying the spoil and the shale
from down by the pit,
across the black bridge
and all the way up to the top of the tip.
Number seven,
that's the one they're going to now.

Even if you were there though,
on the mountain I mean,
you'd still only hear them,
wouldn't see them, not til the cranes at least.

3

Not with this fog like a cloud in the street.
It's dark but I can still tell it's thick.
The way the streetlights blur out
and how I can't see the ridge.
If I could, that would be darker again,
like ink spilt on ink.
And above it, just, the moon,
a harvest one in a week or two.

His older brother WILL stirs under his covers.

Will says they'll be putting a man on it soon.
He means the Americans, but I don't know.
I think the Russians might get there first.
They're launching Luna 12 tomorrow.
Dad told me about it, showed me a picture.
Like a spinning top it is with spikes all over.
Putting it into orbit, if they can.
That's what Dad said –
'Like a moon for a moon, but made by man.'

DAI DAVIES ascends in a cage from deep in the mine.
A chant of miners' nicknames grows under his speech.
With each name uttered a new voice is added.

DAI

Mad about science my Tomos,
always following them rockets.
Which is fine by me.
Better by far he's looking up there

Danny Cold Blood
Dilwyn Hook and Eye
Will One Song
Georgie Pub
Dai Fat
Dai Sweat

to the darkness of space,
than down to the blackness
of this bloody place.

Bob Bad Luck
Ianto Aye Aye
Willy Want
Jack the Black

When DAI speaks again his voice is older, remembering.

DAI

What still haunts me the most
is how it was staring us in the face.
Not just the thing itself
but even the word – Tip.
Pit, turned inside out, wrong way round,
which is how it was, of course.
I was the one meant to be in danger.
It was miners who died for coal,
hundreds each year.
Us in that daytime night,
not our children aboveground
learning in the light.

Tommy Tin Hat
Tommy Duck Egg
Tommy Dunkirk
Colin Sooty
Totty Watkins
Blondie Morgan
Dickie Bach
Dickie Drunk

The colliery hooter sounds.

TOMOS

That's the pit,
sounding the end of the safety shift.

Dai Shake Hands
Will Bumble
Dai Lot of Kids

The sound of an engine.

And that's the bus,
Merthyr Col. on its side
getting ready to give
the next lot a ride.

Slogger Carpenter
Jeff Jaffa
Euchin Cute
Bomper Jackson

DAI strips off his helmet, lamp, belt.

DAI

Never see daylight, not in winter,
not less you're carried out
on a stretcher.

TOMOS

That's what my dad says.
He's down there, see?
But coming up now.
He'll wash, change,

DAI is in the showers, washing off the coal dust.

DAI

and if it's been hot,
screw my vest into my Tommy box.

TOMOS

Then he'll catch the bus back
to have breakfast together.

DAI dries himself, gets dressed.

DAI

It's important, isn't it?
To eat round the table as one.

Otherwise what's the point
of having fathers, a mother, sons?

MYFANWY DAVIES is in her kitchen.

MYFANWY

Might get to eat three times today.
Together I mean. Half-term, so short hours isn't it?
So yeah, Tom'll be home long before tea.

TOMOS upstairs, is getting dressed.

TOMOS

And then tomorrow, a whole week off.
I can't wait.
I'm playing piano at a wedding first thing,
Eine Kleine Nachtmusik
for our neighbours, Sheryl and Colin.
Then, hopefully,
I'll be in time for the films down at Bugs.
Cartoons, then *Riders of Death Valley*.
Then Will said he'd take me to the game –
the Martyrs, not Wales versus Scotland –
playing down in Penydarren.
They beat Ramsgate last week, three–nil,
with Dudley Price at six.

WILL, ecstatic at a match.

WILL

'A bloody angel on that ball!'

TOMOS

That's what Will said when he scored.
'Thank god,' a man said behind,
'he didn't go to Barry Town after all.'

At the other end of the village another set of curtains opens.
ANNE JONES, aged nine, looks out of her bedroom window.
She watches JACK-THE-MILK doing his deliveries.
When she speaks it is with the voice of a 60-year-old woman.

ANNE

I still feel guilty about it.
Silly, I know, but I do.
Because I can remember so clearly,
thinking that morning
as Jack did his rounds in the van,
how nothing new or nothing exciting
ever happened in Aberfan.

Lots going on but always the same,
or for someone else, not me.
That's how it felt.
Busy in the street, the fields,
the pit, but never moving.

Mind you, I was only nine,
so maybe that's it.
And we lived at the top end,
which was poorer.
But I wanted to be like my sister,
older – to listen to the juke box

down Emanuelli's café,
with the boys from Bedlinog
straight-backed on their motorbikes
winking through the window
to take me away.

I wanted something to change
for life to go faster, for me and the village.
But now? – now I just wish
I'd somehow slowed time
not made it go quicker.
Stopped it even,
and with it, that slippage.

IRENE JONES, ANNE's mother, calls up the stairs.

IRENE

Barbara!
You out the bathroom yet?
Get in there Anne, if she is!
Half an hour to get yourself set.

*ANNE turns from the window,
her voice a nine-year-old girl's.*

ANNE

Last day of school today,
then half-term!
If it's fine tomorrow
I might go help on the farm.
Or play up the mountain,

or tag, or hide and seek
up the old canal bank.

But that's tomorrow.
Should think of today.
That's what Mam would say.
Still a morning of school.
Maths, English, then break.
Might play French skipping
if Beth brings her rope.

> *BARBARA, ANNE's older sister,*
> *enters the bedroom, humming a pop song.*
> *The sound of JACK-THE-MILK delivering*
> *can be heard as ANNE goes into the bathroom.*

ANNE

That's Jack-the-Milk, going door to door.
He'll have already been out for an hour,
maybe more.
We usually pass him on the way up to school,
still delivering all down Moy Road,
with Bryntaf and Aberfan Mawr
still to go.

> *ANNE closes the door and looks in the mirror.*

ANNE

Jack.
No father should witness what he saw.
Can't help but ask why, can you?

10

Why his girl, not me?
Why at that moment,
when so many couldn't,
he had to see?

JACK-THE-MILK, out on the street, waves to a neighbour.

DAI is on the colliery bus.

DAI

Like the valley's still asleep
when the mist's down this deep.
But it isn't – never really quiet this village.
One shift coming up, another going down.
Farmers on the hill out for their stock,
mothers stoking the grates,
kids getting ready, trying not to be late.

MYFANWY DAVIES is lighting her fire.

MYFANWY

Then shop deliveries soon.
Busy place, see?
Which is good, of course.
God knows, others have got it worse.
We've still got the mine for one.
And the factories:
ICM, Lines Toys, GKN,
Hoover of course –
So yeah, plenty going round to pay the rent.

DAI gets off the colliery bus.

DAI

Boys from here, I tell you,
they got it better than their fathers,
walking straight out of school into steady employment.

EDNA, a farmer, is out on the hill above the village.

EDNA

Wasn't always like this, of course.
Summer grazing, that's what
brought the first people here.
Good land, sheltered spot,
fed by six streams at least.
It's all still here, in a way,
in the names, the streets.
Hafod Tanglwys –
the summer place of Tanglwys.
Bryn Golau – hill of light.
Pantglas – the green hollow,
and still is I suppose,
though with kids now not grass.
And *Aberfan*, of course –
the mouth of the Fan,
the biggest of those streams
feeding the Taff.

*MYFANWY prepares breakfast,
the sound of her boys dressing above her.*

MYFANWY

Was the steam coal what changed all that.
And John Nixon.
He's still here too, other side of the Taff.
Nixonville it's called,
though far as I can see whole place is that man's.
I mean, was him who started the pit,
and the pit what made Aberfan.

DAI approaches his home.

DAI

From up north he was. Newcastle way.
Saw Merthyr coal burned on the Thames one day,
and couldn't believe it.
No smoke in the coal – never seen that before.
So he came down here looking for more.
Went to Mrs Thomas he did, up at the Graig.
There she was, sitting in her hut
at the mouth of the shaft,
a basket by her head for the cash,
girls sorting by hand outside.
150 tonnes a day she was selling.
But no more.
That's what she told Nixon.
Reckoned she'd taken too much already
out from under the valley's floor.

MYFANWY

But Nixon? Well, he was modern,
didn't understand the words 'Too much'.

> *JOHN PHILLIPS, a crane driver, stands on the summit of*
> *tip number seven, high and isolated in the morning mist.*

JOHN

So he sunk his own – the deepest so far –
then worked his way south, from Navigation
to Deep Duffryn, to here, Merthyr Vale.
He'd proved it, see?
That 10 hours of fire from Aberdare
was worth 12 at least from the Tyne.

DAI

By the time I left school
there seemed no question. The war was over
and my father, well, he was suffering from dust.
So I went down – twenty years next month.
Mrs Thomas would turn, I bet,
to think we're still digging it out.

> *DAI reaches his home.*
> *Above him, TOMOS waves from his window.*

DAI

Generations down that pit.
Not my boys though.
I'm working down there, so they won't.

Will's heading for an apprentice at JJ's garage
and well, according to some he's got a chance in the ring.
And Tomos bach, he's good with his hands too,
in a different way. Only nine,
but plays piano with both of them.

DAI enters his house. MYFANWY takes his coat.

MYFANWY

And now look at us.
Shops, if you could see them in this mist,
from one end of the village to the other.

Shopkeepers begin opening their stores, putting out stock.

You watch, any minute now
those awnings'll start coming down,
like a high street flotilla.

With each shop mentioned a chorus of voices grows.

MYFANWY & CHORUS

Post office,
tailor's,
the Aberfan,
the Mack.
The co-op,
Maypoles,
Barbara's Boutique.
Shoe shop,
the jeweller's,

A man turns in his bed.

MYFANWY

Georgie the barber's.

ANNE comes back into her bedroom.

ANNE

One of the dinner ladies knew my mam!
I mean, when she was little and in Pantglas too.
They're not like the teachers, see,
They're softer, will hold a hand.
And they know everyone, not just the child,
but their *Tad Cu*, their Nan, the whole family.

IRENE is preparing breakfast downstairs.

IRENE

She's right, they do.
Which is good, isn't it?
I mean, to know your daughter's in a place
where they know more than just her face.
Not like down Cardiff
where you're just one in a queue.
On your own. No belongings,
no names behind you.

She looks out the kitchen window to the back garden
where her husband, GWYN JONES is pruning his roses.

IRENE

Take my Gwyn. 'Gwyn the rose'
they call him round here.
Famous for his flowers.
Someone knocks at least once a week,
thumb in their button hole
after a five-leaf.
Gives him a pride, to be known like that.
Had an accident, see? Down the pit.
Works in Hoover's now.
He's had his fair share, fair play –
so those roses, well,
they add to him don't they?

GWYN looks up from his rose bushes.
When he speaks his voice is that of a man in his nineties.

GWYN

I stopped growing them after.
Or least, let them go wild,
stopped cutting them back.
Didn't seem right.
And flowers, well,
they changed for me too.
Whenever I saw them,
in a window, a vase,
I'd see the cemetery slope again,

spread like a quilt.
A quilt of flowers for our village dead.

> *IRENE calls upstairs again.*

IRENE

Anne! You getting dressed up there?
Never mind half day, you know the rules –
school's still school.

She's a dreamer that one.
Youngest of six and youngest by far.
Gets them yearning too soon.
I mean, when their brothers and sisters
are all in their teens.
But I say to her – 'Anne, you cherish these days,
cos believe me, cariad,
one blink, and the world'll make you old
in a hundred ways.'

> *Upstairs, ANNE is plaiting her hair in a mirror.*

ANNE

One blink, and the world'll make you old
in a hundred ways.

IRENE

Anne! Come on!

BARBARA pushes ANNE from the mirror.
Taking her place, BARBARA puts on her make-up.

BARBARA

Last day for me too,
so I'll be out tonight.
The Bystanders playing down Troedyrhiw.
I saw them in the Social last month,
like the Beatles and Moody Blues, all in one.
Bit of soul, bit of Motown.
From Merthyr they are.
We helped them, after, to carry their kit
back up to the train in the Vale.

I got to carry the guitar.
He kissed me for it! The guitarist.
Just on the cheek, but, well,
I think Will Davies saw, got a bit jealous.
It's Amen Corner tomorrow,
according to Sue,
playing down the Queen's café.
She said Will's planning to go, so yeah,
I'll be going to that one too.

She looks out the window at the mist.

Wish this bloody mist would burn off soon.
Least it's stopped raining I suppose.
Old women and sticks it was last night,
streaming black all down the gwlies.

She turns back to the mirror.

But we were used to that, see?
The colour of coal in our water, our river.
Was all we'd ever known.
Those tips were just there,
part of home.
So no, we didn't see
any wrong in that rain.

*The DAVIES family are sitting round the table for breakfast.
Jim Reeves' 'Distant Drums' plays on the radio.*

MYFANWY

Where in Troedyrhiw?

WILL

The Boys' Club. Jeff's going too.

DAI

The Bystanders? Never heard of them

WILL

Yes you have. Merthyr boys.
They played the Democratic Social?

DAI

Oh, yeah. Not my cup of tea.

MYFANWY

What time?

WILL

Starts at eight.

MYFANWY

Home by nine?

WILL

Nine!

DAI

What about training?

WILL

Eddie says we'll be done by seven.
Howard's in after that.

MYFANWY

Eddie! The Merthyr Marvel!
You know he used to deliver our coal?

WILL

You always say that!
Doesn't take away his European title,
that's still a fact.

MYFANWY starts clearing the plates.
She kisses each of her men on the top of their heads.

MYFANWY

Right, come on you two.
Will, you'd better get ready,
and Tomos – time for school.
And you, off to bed. I'll wake you for lunch.

MYFANWY is left on her own.

MYFANWY

I reckon there's a girl at that gig.
I could be wrong, just a hunch.
But never seen Will so keen.
Should be thankful I suppose –
that it's only the Boys' Club,
and not down in Merthyr.
Become like a Mecca, that place,
a jam pot for the wasps.
Every other door a pub,
and the dance halls going full swing.
The Palace, the Kirkhouse . . .

IRENE is in her kitchen, also clearing away, washing up.

IRENE

Like we didn't do the same!
Remember that summer 'Fan?

Heading down Barry
with the small coal charabanc?

MYFANWY

All right, fair dos. Just saying.
Teenagers today, I don't know, it's not the same.
Those charabancs though,
they haven't changed.
Six or seven buses, all in convoy.
The kids, playing on the beach.
Half their fathers up the shops, putting on bets.
Then the long drive back,
with Tomos on me, asleep,
the smell of the sea in his hair,
the grit of the sand in his toes.
Yeah, he still loves going on those,
all the kids do. I mean, it's the ocean –
got to beat swimming down the Taff,
or like we used to,
in the streams under the tips,
hasn't it?

BETTY, SUZY'S mother, is getting SUZY ready for school.

BETTY

Not that here isn't a good place for them.
Loads to do! Always out on the street,
or up the mountain. That's a playground in itself.

IRENE

Anne loves going up there to play hide and seek.

MYFANWY

And Tomos. Sits on cardboard to slide down the tips.

BETTY

We could do without those, granted.
But they're as old as the village, aren't they?

MYFANWY

And the cost to remove them, well,
they reckon it would close the pit,
that's what the N.C.B. said.

IRENE

Plenty else for them down here anyway.

BETTY

The Boys' Club cross country – they're doing well,
beat the British champions just last Saturday.

MYFANWY

And we do all right too, don't we?
Got our own dance hall in the Welfare.

CATRIN, ROB'S mother, is seeing ROB off to school.

CATRIN

When it isn't flooded.

IRENE

And the cinema above it.

CATRIN

Cast a Giant Shadow showing this week.

BETTY

All the clubs – and not just for the men.

IRENE

The United Sisterhood, the Darby and Joan –

> *All four MOTHERS appear with other women*
> *in a line-up for a club photo.*
> *They speak from within the group.*

MYFANWY

– and the Women's League,
that's mine.

IRENE

So, yeah, a good place to be, Aberfan.
And even more so now, with work in the town.

CATRIN

I know gas is pushing a decline
but my mam, she remembers the strike.
Used to tell me, how she'd spread on butter
with two runs of the knife,
once to put it on, then back to take it off again.

MYFANWY

So yes, not a bad place, and not a bad time.
Can't complain.

> *All the women smile.*
> *A flash as the photo is taken –*
>
> *MYFANWY is back in her kitchen.*
> *TOMOS comes down the stairs with his schoolbag*
> *and leaves through the front door.*

TOMOS

Bye Mam.

MYFANWY

Bye, love.

She turns from the door, her voice old again.

MYFANWY

And that's how they went.
Out a hundred doors for their last days.
And that's how we said our last goodbyes,
with all the luxury of easy time.
But it was already draining,
running out like sand in the glass,
like that pile of tailings and shale,
already moving, pressed to a shifting
under the weight of its own black hand.
Restless with rain, storm water.
And under it, on their way to school,
my son.

IRENE is in her kitchen, alone.

IRENE

My daughter.

MYFANWY looks back at the shut front door.

MYFANWY

Bye.

    Love.

TOMOS is walking to school.

TOMOS

I used to walk to school with my mam,
but I go alone now.
Well, not alone, but with my friends,
Robert and Dan.

DAN is walking to school from another direction.

DAN

It's my birthday soon,
the week after we're back.
Mam's said I can have a party,
if I keep on track.

TOMOS

Dan's cousins have got a farm, up the mountain.
Llewellyn and Islwyn.
They let us go and play up there.

DAN

Making swings from the ropes in the yard,
picking apples from off the Plantation.
Got to be careful though.
They've got a bull, see. Called Nelson.

TOMOS

'Nasty piece of work,' that's what my dad says.

'Looks like he'd charge you down
if you let him.'

DAN

I find him fine. But then Islwyn says
as I've got the knack –
farming in my blood, he reckons,
however far back.
So that's what I want to be when I'm older.
A farmer up on the hill.
'Keep up high', that's what Islwyn says.
'Then you know where you are,
nothing in the way
between you and the sky.'

ROB is also walking to school.

ROB

My brother bought a TV this summer,
to watch the World Cup on.
Everyone came round for the final –
our front room, it was like the Mack
on a Saturday night – packed out,

TOMOS

And us all licking our lion-shaped lollies.

ROB

That's when I knew.
I'd be a footballer too.

29

Start with the Martyrs, then play for Wales.
Dad's taking me to the game tomorrow,
against Scotland, down Ninian Park.
He's got us tickets from Merthyr Vale –
the 1.04 gets us there for the start.

DAN

And it did, the 1.04.
Though arrived almost empty.
The match went ahead.
A one-all draw,
Ron Davies scoring with a nifty hack,
the arms of the Welsh team,
banded in black.

TOMOS

That was amazing that world cup final!
When that last goal went in,
well, might have been England,
but we still all made one hell of a row –

ROB

Went crazy!
'They think it's all over . . .

TOMOS is joined on a street corner by ROBERT and DAN.

TOMOS, ROBERT, DAN

'. . . it is now!'

ANNE is waiting for the school bus
with her friends SUZY and BETH.

ANNE

I love this time of year,
I think it's my favourite.
Harvest festival, Bonfire Night.
Then after half-term,
we start rehearsing the play.

SUZY

Do you remember that Bonfire Night
when they gave us all candles?

BETH

Whole street had one,
walking in a line all through the village.

SUZY

A 'river of lights',
that's what my mam said it was like.

TOMOS, DAN and ROB are passing Aberfan Road,
the high street.

TOMOS

Sometimes, if we're early
we'll go into Maypoles –
a grocer's on the high street,
just past the butcher's.

DAN

Not cos we're hungry,

ROB

Or cos we need anything,

TOMOS

But just to watch their bobbins,
strung up on a string.

ROB

More like a zip-line it is.
One push from the counter –

DAN

– and off they go, to the register

TOMOS

Where the cashier takes the money,
puts the change back in,

ROB

then pushes it back to where it began.

TOMOS

Imagine – if we could build that
up on the farm,
a zip-line, not just a swing.

As they carry on past Aberfan Road –

DAN

That morning, though, we were late,
so didn't go to Maypoles,
but Anderson's instead –
a tuck shop on the hill
next to Georgie the barber's.

TOMOS is ordering sweets at the counter –

TOMOS

Three shrimps please,
and two flying saucers.

DAN

Georgie was still in bed,
his shop sign turned to 'closed'.
He's always said – if it had been the other way round,
well . . . let's just say he's grateful he dozed.

As the boys leave Anderson's –

ROB

Listen.

TOMOS

To what?

ROB

The birds. They aren't singing.

DAN

How can you listen to nothing?

TOMOS

It's this mist, isn't it?

ROB

What about it?

TOMOS

Can't see can they?
So don't know it's day.

DAN

It was true.
The mist was still lying heavy,
so as we walked up to school,

just a few steps apart
and we'd lose sight of each other.
If only I'd have known.
I'd have made sure to stay closer.

ANNE, SUZY and BETHAN are on the bus –

BETHAN

Do you think Mrs Jennings
will still make us go out?
Even if at break, it's still like this?

> **SUZY**
>
> You know her rule –
> outside, whatever the weather.

ANNE

What shall we play if she does?
Hopscotch? Tag? Stuck in the mud?

> **SUZY**
>
> L.O.N.D.O.N.
> spells London?

BETHAN

Or Dickie five stones,
or Ginger Ginger, maybe later?

MRS JENNINGS stands at the top of the school steps.
As she watches the buses arrive
other children are left at the gate by their mothers
or walk up to the school in groups.

MRS JENNINGS

I'm sure the children think I'm tough
and probably some of the parents too.
But it's not about governing with fear.
No, it's about being fair.
To them, their futures.
I mean, half these boys are headed for the mine,
and most of the girls for running a house.
But whatever they do,
it's my job to see they do it well.
Good families in this valley,
but no one here has it easy.
Sowing the seeds, that what's done here.
Preparing the crop, year after year.

TOMOS, ROB and DAN approach the school
along Moy Road.

ROB

You know what my dad said last night,
about Mr Beynon?

TOMOS

That he'd beat him in a fight?

DAN

That he's in love with Miss Jones?

ROB

No! That he used to play for Aberdare,
years ago.
At lock he was, and one of their best.

DAN

I could believe it. Huge he was.
I still remember, standing at his feet,
my head well under his chest,
looking up, saying 'sir?'
and thinking, 'Duw,
he goes on for ever!'

MR BEYNON is in his classroom, preparing.

MR BEYNON

They've been good to me, the kids.
I mean, I must be quite an imposition.
One minute Mr Evans is their master,
their deputy head,
then suddenly it's me instead.
That must be hard.
A stroke. A couple of weeks ago.

He's on the mend though, from what I can tell.
The children sent him a card.
People forget, I think, when they grow older,
just how fond a class can get of their teacher.
Can't say I'm quite there yet.
But then it always takes time, doesn't it?

> *The children arrive at the school gates.*
> *JACK-THE-MILK is delivering in the street behind them.*
> *He waves to his daughter.*

ANNE

We had assembly that day.
The whole school, sitting cross-legged
on the parquet floor.

DAN

The whole school, ages five to ten,
singing 'All Things Bright and Beautiful'.

ANNE

No. 'There Is a Green Hill Far Away'.
That's what we sang.
I think. I can't be sure.

DAN

Then we went to our classes,
that I do know.
Each age through a different door.

ANNE

I sat by a window. I remember that.
Mr Davies up front, writing the date.

> **MR DAVIES**
> October the . . .?
> Come on, who can tell me?

>> *TOMOS is at his desk.*

> **TOMOS**
> Sir?

>> **MR DAVIES**
>> Yes, Tomos?

TOMOS

20th August, 1963.
Dear Sir,
RE:

>> *Anne joins in.*

ANNE & TOMOS

Danger from coal slurry being tipped at the rear
of Pantglas school, Aberfan.

> *Two more children join in the recitation.*

In connection with the above
my public works Superintendent
has been in touch with Mr Wynne,

Four more children join.

Manager at the Merthyr Vale Colliery
in connection with the deposit of slurry

Eight more children join.

on the existing tip at the rear
of the Pantglas school.

Sixteen more children join.
The whole class is now reciting the letter.

I am very apprehensive about this matter
as are the councillors and the residents in this area
as they have previously experienced,
during periods of rain,
movement of the slurry
to the danger and detriment
of people and property
adjoining the site of the tips.

Thirty-two villagers join the voices of the children.

13th December, 1963.
Dear Sir,
RE: Danger from coal slurry being tipped at the
rear of Pantglas school, Aberfan.

As a matter of emergency ...

Sixty-four more voices from the village join.

I feel it is necessary
that the N.C.B. be made to commit ...
without any delay ...
in the event of the tips ...

EDNA, still on the hill, adds her voice.

31st January, 1964
Dear Sir,
RE:

EDNA'S young child joins with her.

In spite of what the Area Engineer
says in his letter of 28th January ...

EDNA'S husband also joins.

... I am not of the opinion that further material
is unlikely to be washed
down the waterway

*A gang of nine workers at the summit
of tip number seven join in.*

... on the 22nd January I stated that the pipes

Another two tip workers add their voices.

under the Aberfan road were half full of silt

Another two workers join,
bringing the total voices speaking to 144.

and that conditions were ripe ...

One of the workers, JOHN, a crane driver, speaks.

JOHN

When we arrived that morning,
it was still quite dark, but we could all still see,
the point of the tip, it had sunk.
The track for my crane had fallen in,
slipped from where it should be.
I asked Dave, one of the slingers,
to run on down,
let Les our charge-hand know.
Which he did.
There used to be a telephone,
but the wires, they kept getting stolen.
So Dave went down instead.
I watched him fade and go.
The mist, you see, it was cloud-cover thick.
We couldn't see the village below.

The recitation of the letters continues,
without the voices of the workers.

So far as the council are concerned
there has been a deterioration
in the position

EDNA'S husband drops out.

```
As I have said ...
the silt washed down ...
```

EDNA'S child drops out.

```
will now build up ...
```

EDNA speaks alone.

EDNA

I'd been out in that mist,
so thick I could only see
a couple of the poles down below,
the ones that carry the wires into town.
One, two, maybe three, no more.
Then suddenly, those wires,
they started swinging around,
started jumping.
Like some giant hand
was playing at skipping.

In the village 128 voices continue.

```
I respectfully suggest that you require the
submission ...
in order to safeguard the future position ...
```

Sixty-four voices leave.

```
I have not yet had
a satisfactory reply
to the questions raised.
... sliding in the manner
that I have envisaged.
```

Thirty-two voices in the school fade away.

```
I understand ...
... that the slurry is de-watered
before being tipped
but... this would not be a solution
to movement in winter time due
```

Sixteen more children drop out.

```
to the absorption of storm water.
```

Eight more children fall silent.

```
You are no doubt aware
of the tips
above Pantglas
```

Four more children leave.

```
and if they were to move
```

Two more children stop speaking,
leaving just TOMOS and ANNE.

TOMOS & ANNE

a very serious position

ANNE drops out.

TOMOS

would accrue.

MR DAVIES

Yes, Tomos?

TOMOS

October 21st, 1966. Sir.

*MR DAVIES writes the date on the blackboard
ANNE raises her hand.
There is a faint rumbling sound.*

ANNE

Sir?

MR DAVIES

Yes?

ANNE

Is that thunder?

MR DAVIES

Maybe, Anne.

45

ANNE

But then it got louder than thunder ever can.
And faster.
I looked out the window, saw Jack-the-Milk,
then – and I still don't know why,
I had no time to think –
I put the book I was reading over my head.
Seconds later, the darkness came in,
as if all the eyes in all the world,
had chosen then to blink.

A single milk bottle falls, breaks.
The rumble becomes a roar,
increasing in volume.

PART II

Rescuers

In every window

The roaring becomes the sound of tyres on tarmac.
Car headlights on an empty motorway.
A young medical student, MANSEL, is at the wheel.

MANSEL

I'm a scientist, so I don't
believe in spirits and such.
But I've always kept a diary,
a page of A4, every night,
so it's there, in black and white.

We couldn't sleep. Me or my wife.
We were living, back then,
in East London. Us and our baby boy,
but that wasn't where we were from.
No, that was Merthyr and Aberfan.
And that's where we were going
in the early dark that morning.

A christening, later that day.
Like I said, we couldn't sleep.
No point lying in bed, awake,
that's what we thought.
So we packed up the Ford,
and went.

DAVE EVANS is in his home in Aberfan.
As he speaks he answers the door to a NEIGHBOUR.

DAVE

I was getting ready for work,
up at the bank.
Hadn't long put on my suit and tie
when a neighbour came over,
asked if he could use our phone.
He seemed upset.
'Of course,' I said. 'Why?'

NEIGHBOUR

There's something wrong.
A house has collapsed, up at Moy Road.

DAVE EVANS

Collapsed? How?

NEIGHBOUR

That's all I was told.
But it's happened, just now.

DAVE EVANS

So I dialled, 999.
Got through to the fire service
and let them know.
While I was on the line
I heard a woman scream. I looked up.

Men were running past my window.

(*on the phone*)
I think it's something major.
How long til you arrive?

OPERATOR

As soon as we can.
Your call's been logged at 09.25.

*SAM KNIGHT, a young journalist,
is sitting on the train.*

SAM

I'd just got back from honeymoon.
A week near Burnham Beeches.

I was still living in Cardiff
with my wife and her parents.

I was young, ambitious,
been at the *Express* for a year and a half.

I wanted to go places, travel.
And I did.

But that morning, it was just Merthyr again,
on the train –

an early interview with the council's John Beale,
Director of Education.

After, as I was coming down the steps
of his offices,

a car pulled up at the kerb –
one of the paper's photographers,

Mel Parry, only eighteen back then,
been to the station for the morning call.

> *MEL winds down his window.*

MEL

There's been a couple of incidents –
a domestic fire in Dowlais,
or an outhouse collapsed at the school in Aberfan.
Which do you think?

SAM

Fires are common enough,
let's try the school.
Sounds a bit different.

So I got in, and Mel drove on.

MEL

We were approaching Merthyr Vale
when we saw the cars in the mist.
A chain of headlights,
blue and red stitched
with police, an ambulance.

All coming towards us,
away from Aberfan.
I watched them pass,
become a river of red in our mirror.

SAM

'Something serious has happened,'
I said to Mel.
He gave a nod, no more,
and like that, against the headlight flow
and our own tyres' hiss, we drove on,
in silence, into that mist.

GWYNETH LEWIS is in the Mayor's office.

GWYNETH

I'd been Mayor's secretary
since March of '66.
I'd got in early that morning.
We'd lit the fire
and the switchboard girl
had been in to turn her handle.
All was normal.

Then, suddenly, the men were leaving.

They'd been told, you see, to go to Aberfan.
The offices emptied, to a man.
Just the women left.
No one could tell us why.
We didn't know what to do.

But then the ambulances
started streaking through town,
and we knew.
Within the hour
we'd gone from staffing the office
to a crisis HQ.

MANSEL

It must have been around 9.30,
as we reached Dowlais Top,
when out of the mist
we saw a road block.
I pulled up.

A POLICE OFFICER approaches the car.

OFFICER

Which way you going?

> MANSEL

> Brecon Road, in Merthyr.

Which is when he said.

A disaster.
That's what he called it, even then.

Of course, we thought it was the pit.
All my father's side is from Aberfan,
and always been miners too.
And my wife's family,
they ran a shop in the village.

The officer was about to signal us on,
when he saw the sticker
above my bumper – B.M.S.A.

> > OFFICER

> > Are you a doctor?

> > MANSEL

> > A student. Final year.

> OFFICER

> But you're medical?
> We could use your help if so.
> All the other doctors, see? They're up
> at St Tydfil's for the casualties,
> or in Merthyr Central.

MANSEL

Of course. Anything I can do.

And that was it. They waved us through.

DAVE is out on the street, crowds running past him.

DAVE

I followed the crowd running down my street,
turned at the Mack and couldn't believe it.
They're making a film – that's all I could think.

The apex of the roofs, you see,
they were, well, all sitting on rubble.
Everything else had gone.

And then, as I looked, that rubble wept.
The Cardiff to Merthyr main,
burst by the slipping tip.

It just kept on coming,
turning windows to waterfalls
but thick and black, not like water at all.

Most of the crowd carried on to Pantglas,
but I and some others, we stayed where we were.
There was a boy, see? Who we'd found,

an older lad, been walking to school
when the debris came down.
We didn't have tools,

but we still got to him just in time.
Seconds later and the place he'd been caught
was boiling with slurry and grime.

The boy pulled out is WILL DAVIES.

SAM is faced with the full horror of the landslide.

SAM

It looked like the Somme.
That's what I thought
when we came round the corner.

A mountain of slurry with men all over,
like ants, and all of them digging
with their fingers, their hands.

I had my notebook, my pen,
but I couldn't take them out.
So instead, I climbed up on to it,

that mass of underground waste,
and joined a chain
passing back buckets of slurry.

It was only after a bit that I noticed –
it was still moving.
The whole dark body of it,

a slow buckle and seep
like a small coal muscle
hard but supple, flexing under our feet.

More people were coming all the time,
with shovels, picks, spades.
I saw firemen further up

pulling out a man in pyjamas.
In one of the classrooms
a dram was stuck,

that's what someone said,
and animals too, from the farm on the hill –
sheep, a cow, all dead.

MANSEL is at the site of the school.

MANSEL

It sounds odd to say it now
but what it resembled, that scene,
was like something from the gold rush –

like one of those old photos
where every man has staked out his pitch,
to prospect for wealth.

Except these men
were digging for something else
and for something more precious too –

their little ones.
Their sons, daughters, nephews, nieces
still stuck in that school.

I walked on into it all,
the slurry like dark cement,
asked if I could help.

But there was no one to treat,
that's what the local GP said.
At least, not yet, not from under the rubble.

Soon enough though, those diggers
were getting into trouble.
Most had never worked so hard in their life,

so began collapsing with pains in their chests.
I did my best to see them right,
treated sprains, cuts – but it wasn't enough.

How could it be, in that landscape of pain?
With that great black tongue
lolling out of the mist,

and just there, nearby, the mothers
holding each other, knee-deep in the grit,
looking on at what that slipping tip had done.

> *Among the mothers are*
> *MYFANWY, IRENE, BETTY, CATRIN*
> *all waiting around the school gates.*

DAVE

Soon enough, every able man was
working to clear it.
Some children had been pulled out alive,
but everyone knew, we didn't have much time.
I heard lorries and turned to see
the miners, up from the colliery.
Hundreds of them, jumping off before

those lorries had stopped
and diving straight in to attack that slip,
that pile of waste they'd once dug from the pit.

A chant of miners' names runs under the rest of his speech.

God did they work. And organised us too.
Had teams digging trenches,
others making corrugate chutes.
Every now and then a cry would go up
and to a man, we'd all still and listen.
Machines would stop –
breaths were held –
until the source of the sound was found
and then a fury of digging again.

Johnny Howler
Eddie Dixie
George Aberdare
Will Bumble
Dai Gold Watch
Jones Merthyr Vale
Cocker Nash
Dai Stonedust
Bill Bird's Eye

Until around eleven.
When for the first time that day
hundreds of us listened,
leant on our shovels, straining every sense,
only to be met
with nothing but silence.

Billy Iron Boot
Freddie Greenfly
Dai Lamplight
Tommy Cocoa
Ianto Aye Aye
Cyril Silent Night

MANSEL

I'd taken over with a shovel
when a young man came over.
'We're into a classroom,' he said.

'You'd better come through, just in case . . .'
So I passed my tool to another
and followed him into the ruins of that place.

For years I've had dreams
because of what I saw –
The classroom, it was like it had been shaken.

Desks, chairs, a boulder,
a clock angled where it fell
and there, up against the wall,

no higher than your waist, twenty children,
their master in front of them,
his arms spread in protection,

trying to save them all.
He was a big man but what could he have done?
One teacher against a mountain.

I could see, behind him, their faces,
their mouths still open
as if they'd been caught mid-song.

Except you could tell,
it wasn't a song
those mouths had been making,

all crammed as they were

with the same black note
of shale, slurry and grit.

And their eyes as well.
I've never seen a thing so wrong.
There was nothing to be done.

GWYNETH is gathering with others in the council chamber.

GWYNETH

Around eleven we assembled in the chamber
to be informed of the plans.
'We're setting up mortuaries,' they said.

'Wherever we can.' We were stunned, numb.
But of course, had to carry on.
There was so much to be done.

At around four the women
as well as the men
were asked to go to Aberfan.

Once there we gathered in a hall,
unsure what would happen.
But then John Beale, Director of Education,

he came in, school registers under his arm.
He wanted to account for the children,
so began to read out their names,

but their sound on the air, what it conjured,
was too much for him. He broke down.
And anyway, nobody knew –

who had survived, and who had not.
So each of the women was given a street
and told to go down it from door to door,

asking each family a single question
against the grain of natural law –
I was twenty-two. Each time I knocked

I prayed the answer would be yes, he's here,
or yes, she's asleep upstairs.
But of course, all too often it wasn't.

I'd write down the name, or the names,
the ages – seven, eight, nine.
We'd talk, if they wanted.

Then they'd close their door, softly,
the hand of a husband or wife on their shoulder,
and I'd carry on,

with my list of numbers, names and ages,
willing for it not to grow any longer.

DAVE

As the news filtered into the world
so the world filtered back to us.
Factories emptied across Wales,

steelworkers from Port Talbot,
Hoover down in Merthyr,
schoolboys from a valley over.

And individuals too, a farmer
from Brecon, an accountant from Cardiff,
and many others from further.

And of course the TV crews.
The journalists. First from Wales
then the UK, then France, Germany, all over.

They set up at the Mack,

filmed us working, the slide, the tips,
the chimneys, still smoking through the black.

I heard one reporter ask a miner,

> REPORTER
>
> They say you'll dig into the night,
> is that true?

DAI DAVIES turns to answer.

> DAI
>
> My boy's in there somewhere,
> I'll dig all year if I have to.

DAVE

At some point the N.C.B. rescue teams came.
Like the cavalry they were,
in their yellow jackets and hats.

Then the army, digging trenches
clearing storm water – from all over the country
feather pumps and tenders.

No one else would be pulled out alive.
Not from the houses, nor the school.
But still, all you could hear

was the sound of digging tools.
And, occasionally, quiet crying.
Because now there was other work to do –
supporting the parents at Bethania chapel,

small bodies under blankets on every pew
as they went in to identify their children,

sometimes by face but often
by just a piece of cloth, a pair of shoes.
Somehow, throughout it all,

the workers were fed, watered.
Soup and bread from the Salvation Army,
the Civil Defence. Even, at one point,

a plate of wedding cake.
But then, that's what happens isn't it?
The world ruptures and we offer what we can.

And that's what happened that night,
to a woman and man,
people gave their strength, their sympathy –
offered up, for Aberfan.

SAM

When the day started fading
they brought in arc lights
powered by canisters of gas.

Towers were erected from which they shone
across that whole expanse
of ruin and slurry and black.

Everyone was covered in muck,
me included. I'd worn my best suit
to go and see John Beale

but now you'd have thought
I'd spent the day down the pit.
But we hadn't. It had come to us.

Everyone knew that now.
And when it did, like some heartless pied piper
it harvested the best of that town.

It was time for me to go.
Dusk was giving to night.
I wanted to see my wife.

The Merthyr to Cardiff line had been cut
so I caught a bus.
I was the only one on it, and like that,

held in the brightness of its upper deck,
I travelled home alone, through the darkness,
being sick at my feet as it went.

From what I can't say.
Exhaustion, sadness, who knows.
The body has its ways

of telling when we've had too much.
But as the bus sailed on
down that dark valley

with me, a dirty grain in its light,
even with my eyes closed, being sick,
I couldn't help seeing

one specific sight –

The curtains of a house in a short terraced street
I'd passed earlier that day.

They were closed, which in Wales
not at night, means only one thing –
a house where the seeds of death

have been sown.
I walked on, but as I did
I looked down the rest of that row,

which is when I saw –
the curtains, they were drawn
in every window.

Behind drawn curtains, 116 children's beds lie empty.

PART III

Survivors

And some of that darkness, light

Aberfan, early morning, 2016.
The sound of rumbling wheels gets louder, faster.
TOM, nine years old,
is hurtling down a pavement on his scooter.
Above the valley's ridge turbine blades rise and fall.
In the community centre pool an elderly man swims front crawl.

As TOM rides his scooter through the streets
voices from across the village are heard.

TOM

It's amazing our school.
Got iPads, astro turf
and loads of clubs too.
Science is my favourite.
We've been learning about Tim Peake
all this week.
Six months he was up there!
Mr Davies says tomorrow
we'll see it from here –
the space station. A manmade star,
that's what'll be like,
passing just above the ridge,
slow, but faster than a satellite.

MARK, the community centre manager,
walks barefoot beside the pool.

MARK

I'd say of the names
who come through the door
I know about 80 per cent.
And behind the names too.
Most call it a leisure centre
but for me, well, I'd rather
see it as a talking one.
It counts for a lot, doesn't it?
That bouncing off each other.

RHIAN, a beautician,
turns on lights in the Serenity Beauty Salon.

RHIAN

I'll be honest, at first I wasn't sure,
I mean, how a salon would go down in Aberfan?
How wrong was I?
Within a week of opening
I'd done half the nails in town.

Mothers and toddlers arrive at Trinity daycare.

MOTHER

My two, they love it here.
It's just the best in the area.
Get loads of mums from elsewhere too –
Merthyr, Aberdare, Troedyrhiw.

A postman walks along Moy Road.

POSTMAN

It's how a place gets known, isn't it?
In all seasons.
I mean, however fine, you only ever see it true
if you've known it in other weathers too,
under rain, mist.
I mean, that's when a place shows isn't it?
In the lifting, the burning through.

> *MEGAN, nine years old,*
> *is in her room getting ready for school.*

MEGAN

Now dancing's more my thing –
Cha-cha, Jive, Latin.
I play football too,
in a mixed team run by the Social.
Unless it's tipping,
then I'll stay inside,
listen to One Direction.

> *MRS MANN is pulling up the shutters at the village shop.*

MRS MANN

It just looked so beautiful,
when we first drove in.
We thought it would be
a good place for the kids.
And we were right.
It's scenic, quiet.

They feel safe, even at night.

> *SIMONE, headmistress at Ynysowen school,*
> *arrives at her office.*

SIMONE

When it comes to aspiration,
there's just so much to be done.
I mean, education – for most
it's the one shot they've got,
so yeah, we've got to get it right.

> *TOM arrives at the house of his grandmother, ANNE.*
> *When she opens the door a photograph can be seen in the hallway.*
> *It is of her as a schoolgirl with her friends BETHAN and SUZY.*
> *TOM and ANNE leave for his school,*
> *TOM on his scooter, ANNE walking behind.*

TOM

When Mam and Dad start early,
Mam Gu takes me in.
Dad's on the new builds, see?
Up Merthyr.
And Mam's up there too,
at the call centre.

> *At the school SIMONE is watching the children arrive.*
> *RHIAN waves to MEGAN as she enters the gates.*
> *ANNE kisses TOM goodbye, then turns to walk*
> *back into the village.*

ANNE

I didn't go to school for about a year after.
None of us did, who'd survived.
They put some caravans

down at the site where the Welsh school is now.
Back then it was a tip –
coal and slag at the sides.

Toys had been donated, books for us to read.
We could stay, leave,
come and go as we pleased.

I didn't live at home, either, for a while.
Went to live with an older sister.
In the street, see, every child

except me, was dead.
So I was difficult
for the other parents to see.

'They took all the roses,'
that's what one woman said to me.
'And left us the thorns.'

So yeah, I went away for a bit.
When I came back my mother
was completely bald.

She'd been on the ambulances,
taking the bodies.
Weeks later her hair fell out.

'You're the lucky one,'

she'd say when I asked after my friends,
'that's all you need to know about.'

In the end they sent us
to Mount Pleasant,
but we were too disruptive,

that's what they say –
the Pantglas kids, and the teachers too.
Every time a train went by

we'd scream, hide under desks and bins.
So then they moved us
to some portakabins,

down by where Trinity is now.
But still, if there was thunder, lightning,
the teachers would shout, tell us to hide.

They were only young themselves
and like us, still traumatised.
So yeah, wouldn't be right

to say those who'd survived
entirely escaped that tip's landslide.
We got out, yes,

and most of us have got on too.
But the shadow of that shale,
those tailings –

it's long and deep, and cast inside.
How could it not be?
We were children,

going to school with our friends
then, minutes later,
climbing out again, without them.

*DAVE, now in his seventies,
is in Megabytes, formally Emanuelli's café.
As he makes himself a coffee –*

DAVE

People came together after.
It was the only way.
A new magazine
did a lot of good work – *Headway*.

Community run, made sure
the same story, at the same time,
got out to everyone.
It's all stood us in good stead, I'd say.

Over forty groups
came together in association.
It's meant from then on,
we've spoken as one, more or less.

Vigilance – that became the watchword,
for the village's wellbeing.
And we've had to be,
because make no doubt

there have been hard times since.
The strike, the mine closing,
drugs ravaging the young.

Then they tried to build a road,

the A470, right through Aberfan.
Well, no way that was going to happen.
Even this place – when the Emanuellis left,
it became a community caff.

Don't get me wrong.
It's not like there hasn't been anger.
Of course there was. Still is.
I remember on the Monday after,

when it first made itself known,
when our silent grief became heard.
It was at an inquest at Zion chapel
into the deaths of thirty of the children.

The coroner, he was reading out the causes –
asphyxia, multiple injuries –
when from out of the crowd
a father, stood.

24 October, 1966 – DAI stands at the inquest.

DAI

No, sir. Buried alive
by the National Coal Board.
That's what I want
on the official record.

DAVE

The coroner, Mr Hamilton,

he paused, and in that silence
a woman cried out –

BETTY at the inquest.

BETTY

They have killed our children!

DAVE

But we had to heal, and I'd say we have.
Whole place is greening back up.
Go up the canal bank, in July, August,
when the thistle heads are seeding,

catching the light, early berries budding,
chaffinches singing.
Well, beautiful it is.
I've always tried to do my bit,

set up a scheme for apprenticeships,
that kind of thing. Can't say why,
because I was there, perhaps,
or because I'm still here.

Or maybe because I've always felt lucky.
My father, see, he was deputy,
at the school, but had a stroke
a few weeks before.

His replacement was Dai Beynon,
a lovely man. And his class,
they sent my father a card.
I found it again, just the other day

and, well, it brought it home again.
Every single child who'd signed,
they'd died, and Dai Beynon too.
Not one left alive.

So yeah, maybe that's why.

WILL, now sixty-six, is entering the community centre gym.

WILL

I let the boxing slip, after.
Somehow didn't seem right.
And well, Mam and Dad,
they needed me at home.

And I needed to be there too.
And I didn't. I mean,
that's where it was hardest I suppose.
Where the space left by Tomos

was most felt, most known.
I won't lie, I went off the rails for a bit.
Lots of us did. And not just the kids.
Studies were done, proved what we knew.

That depression here was higher,
especially among the women, and drinking too.
Hardly a surprise. I mean,
I've had my own daughter since,

so I know. Is there anything more alive
than an eight-, nine-year-old child? No.

So imagine losing all that life at once,
all that talk and song and dance and fight.

Enough to put any place out for the count.
There's one woman I know
still waiting for her girl to come home.
Sits there, every day, watching out the window.

But we got back up, didn't we? That's for sure.
As a village, and on our own.
Me? I took up at JJ's, became a mechanic,
and married Barbara too.

I don't know, we'd always been keen on each other
and even though my brother died
while her sister survived, well, we'd both still lost,
in a way. Maybe that drew us closer, I like to think so.

I still think of my friends every week.
The ones I was with when that slurry
came down the street. The ones who ran
the other way, and just because of that . . .

I think of my brother too, of course.
What type of man he'd have been.
If he'd had kids, in their faces,
how much of him or me we'd have seen.

But you've got to move on haven't you?
Lots happened since then.
Barbara and I are grandparents now!
And our Rhian's doing well.
She's got the salon in here, see?

In the squash court. Had an outside wall –
could never get any speed on the ball,
so they offered it to her, and she went for it.

*SIMONE is standing at the school entrance,
overseeing latecomers.*

SIMONE

They've had some tough decades
these south Wales valleys.
Forty per cent unemployment
and lots of working poor.
So for me, it's about opening the world
to these kids. And their eyes.
Letting them see what they could do,
who they could be.
Because you can only aspire
to what you can imagine, or see.

All that though, the teaching,
running a school,
that comes easily enough to me.
But then there's other stuff
that's harder to negotiate.
Each year, for example,
we mark the disaster's date.
And we should too. But it's difficult,
sometimes, to know exactly what to do.
Some want to talk, to remember,
others, stay quiet, forget.

And here, well, they're just kids,
same age as those who died.
So yes, we teach it, but gently,
as part of the general history.
It's still so close to home for them –
the communal grave in the cemetery,
the plaques on the walls in the centre,
and for some, still there, still alive
in their grandparents' memories.

RHIAN is working in Serenity Salon.
MYFANWY, now eighty, is waiting for her treatment.

RHIAN

Aberfan, it's known isn't it?
Anywhere you go, you say the name
and people are like 'Oh', nodding,
thinking of the disaster.
But that's not the whole story.
I mean, if it was, they must think
we're a miserable place,
sitting round crying, long in the face.
But that's not true.
Take the Young Wives Club.
I know it grew from what happened,
but then it grew beyond it too – I'd say that's fair?
Buses to London, theatre trips,
that's mostly what they do,
from what the ladies tell me in this chair.

MYFANWY

And laughing. Might sound strange but it's true,
and partly why the group was formed.
We felt guilty, see, whether your child
had survived or died,
to be seen laughing in the street or having fun.
But we were human. And hurting terribly,
all of us, which is why it was so vital
to have somewhere we could go
to laugh, cry, have a recital
or just talk, get on a bus and go out,
to forget and remember, together.

It became a way we could offer too,
contribute I mean, in the community.
Meals on wheels, we started those.
Donkey derbies for charity,
entertained the old people,
held keep fit classes – very popular, those –
twenty, thirty of us, all in leotards
doing aerobics in the hall.
And from early on we organised speakers –
on literature, history – and trips as well,
to London on the train,
coming back at three in the morning,
Stratford upon Avon for the R.S.C.
Oh we've been getting some great deals lately!
Went to the opera recently, in Cardiff,
saw *Madam Butterfly*, and *Falstaff*!

DAN, now sixty, is sitting in his home.

DAN

How to talk about it.
That's been a struggle from the very start.
When something like that happens
a village, a person, they're bound to go dark.

They did their best, they really did.
Psychologists offered to the community,
educational and clinical.
But all that, those processes,

they were still in their infancy.
And sometimes, well, right then, straight after,
isn't when you need them.
I remember, for example,

the one appointed to me, he'd say
don't think about bad things,
like what happened,
but happy things, like your birthday.

My birthday! How could he have known?
There was no worse thing.
I'd been looking forward to mine,
Twenty, thirty friends at a party.

But then when the date came
there were only three, four of us about,
and that's when it really sunk in.
My friends, they'd been wiped out.

When the hospital sent me home
playing outside was frowned upon.
I suffered from guilt, bed wetting,
lack of concentration.

So yes, how do you talk about that?
Can you blame anyone
for wanting to shut the world out
and just carry on?

There was, at least, a public conversation.
The funerals first, of course,
a kind of communal speech of grief –
the grave like a trench,

the hearses, the crowds, the flowers.
Even the coffins, allowed home again
the evening before,
so mothers and fathers across Aberfan

might say goodnight, blow a kiss,
close the door on sleep once more.
Then there were the inquests, the tribunal.
Another public conversation

and necessary, I'm sure,
though many found it hard
to settle with its conclusion.
No one prosecuted, no one sacked

nor forced to resign – and with the N.C.B.
claiming no knowledge or sign
of a spring under the tip.

After generations had swum in it.

Corporate manslaughter,
that's what it amounted to.
'Not wickedness but ignorance, ineptitude
and a failure of communication'

that's what the final report claimed,
and that the N.C.B. carried the blame
for a lack of regulation.
But perhaps if good were to come

it was always going to come
from another direction.
From inside, not out.
Here, that meant the forming of groups,

how we've always, in every generation,
had our best conversation –
Not alone, but as one.

> *DAI, now eighty-five, is setting up the rehearsal room*
> *for the Ynysowen Male Voice Choir.*

DAI

I was on the tip removal committee.
Had to be really. Like everyone else
I wanted them gone.
Not surprising, when you think what they'd done.

But after the tribunal they were inspected
and the N.C.B. declared them safe.

No reason to go, that's what they said.
Well, we wouldn't take no.

Because that wasn't the point, was it?
Safe or not (and we'd heard that before)
we didn't want to see them each day
when we opened our doors.

Piles of the stuff on the mountain side,
dug out, for many of us,
by our very own hands.
It took my boy away –

that was reason enough for me.
So we formed the committee.
Towards the end things got a bit militant,
sacks of slurry on the Welsh Secretary's steps,

that kind of thing, but eventually,
they went.
Which is when we were left asking,
what next?

Removing those tips, see? It brought us together,
and in a way, no denying, it helped
and we didn't want that helping to end.
So, we had a meeting and someone said, why not a choir?

Well, I'd always enjoyed singing,
so I was up for it and so were the others,
twelve in total. We chose our name that night too –
Ynysowen, from the phone exchange area,

and set out what we'd do.
Sing only for charity and only for free.
We wanted to say thank you, see?
To all those people and countries

who'd sent donations, who'd let us know
that they were there.
And we've stuck to that plan.
The choir's changed of course, lots of new men,

but that spirit hasn't, still the same.
We've sung the Albert Hall, Hyde Park
on V. E. Day and toured, well,
more than I can say.

Ireland, Scotland, Germany, France,
but England mostly,
the north and the east,
that's where we like to return to the most.

It can be a struggle, of course,
to keep numbers up, and to keep the right mix.
Always been strong in the bass we have,
but tenors, altos, thinner on the ground.

But we're still here, and still singing,
that's the main thing.
And each time we do, well,
I think of it as a tribute of sorts.

To my boy, and his playing with both hands
and, of course, to everyone else who died.
But not just to them.
Also, in a way, to us, the village,
to those who've survived.

ANNE is having a coffee in the community centre café.

ANNE

It was years later, when we were adults,
that we all finally talked about it.
Not just those who'd been pupils in the school,
but the teachers too. Looking back
they were so young as well, just N.Q.T.s,
twenty-two, twenty-three.
We got in touch, said right, let's do this.
Asked each other questions, shared our stories
and got really drunk as we did,
as if it was the only way
we could let everything out.

Since then, I'd say it's been better.
All of us still carry the scars, of course,
and I couldn't help notice,
that none of us, when we met, had held down
relationships – either never married
or had, then divorced.
We'd mostly been successful, though.
A barrister, a writer, an accountant, a mayor –
as if having survived that collapsing pile

we'd made a pact with ourselves
to make the living we'd been given worthwhile.

> *DAN arrives at the Ynysowen Male Voice Choir rehearsals.*
> *Other members are also filtering through the door, rolling the*
> *piano into position.*

DAN

I studied hard, in the end. Went to university
then worked for years in the City.
I felt in a way like I had a duty,
to succeed not just for me, but for my friends as well,
the children in that class
who never got the chance
to be what they hoped, or to even try.

So yeah, I think that's why.

> *The choir mistress calls the choir together.*
> *They begin vocal warm-ups.*

> *MYFANWY is in the Young Wives Club meeting room.*
> *BARBARA, now fifty-six, is also there,*
> *as are IRENE, CATRIN and BETTY.*
> *The session has not yet begun – there is a mutter of general*
> *conversation.*

MYFANWY DAVIES

The club's changed, obviously, over the years.
Just last week, we put it to the vote,

and decided – time to drop the 'young' from our title.
So just the 'Wives Club' now we are.

CATRIN

But that's okay isn't it?
Because, well, it's that depth makes this what it is.
Coming together for fifty years or so
and for many of us, all still carrying that same green hollow.

MYFANWY

I don't know, it's fine by me
if what we were, what we've known,
starts becoming history.

BETTY

Strange though, too, isn't it?
I mean, just last week I took my granddaughter
up the cemetery, to the memorial.
She's learning about it, see? In school.
She looked at the graves, the names
then turned to me, and said
'Is one of these yours, Nan?'
Well, I had to laugh.

IRENE

What did you answer?

BETTY

What could I? Only the truth.

No love, I said. None of these is Nan's.
But they are, in a way, all of ours,
Aberfan's.

> *CATRIN picks up a cut-glass hand bell and rings it*
> *to signal the start of the session.*

CATRIN

If everyone's ready, shall we begin?

At the Ynysowen choir rehearsal WILL has joined his father.
The CHOIR MISTRESS raises her hands and the choir
start to sing.
ANNE is at the playground by the memorial garden,
watching TOM play with MEGAN and other friends.

ANNE

The way I see it, more and more,
is that we're all carbon, aren't we?
At least that's what Tom keeps telling me.

And what happened here,
it was the most terrible weight.
The worst you can imagine.

A weight on lives, families,
the community, the town.
But what happens to carbon under pressure,

if you keep pressing down?
Well, at first, you get coal,
a darkness that burns.

But keep pressing long and hard enough
and some of that coal turns diamond,
and some of that darkness, light.

Now I'm not saying we're all diamonds
here, of course I'm not.
But I do think that when so many

have felt the same pressure
at exactly the same time,
then sometimes, in places,

we're pushed through til we shine –
an unexpected brightness,
made both of that darkness

and that sharing of weight,
its source buried under the years
but there, deeply rooted
in our memories, a day, a date.

> *ANNE'S son, GWYN, approaches up the hill.*
> *He wears a decorator's overalls.*

ANNE

Hello, love.

> *GWYN kisses TOM on the top of the head*
> *then goes on to give ANNE a hug.*
> *His arrival triggers a game among the children.*

BOY

I'm going to be a painter,
like Tom's dad!

TOM

An astronaut! That's what I'm going to be.

MEGAN

A dancer, on *Strictly*!

OTHER CHILDREN

A goalkeeper, for Chelsea.

A pilot, or a hairdresser

A fish-and-chip man

A teacher

An accountant, if I can

A rugby player

*Children from 1966 including TOMOS, ROB, BETHAN and
SUZY join in the game. The calling out of occupations becomes
a pattern of voices from then and now,
a mosaic of lives hoped for and never lived.*

A freerunner

A singer

A soldier

A nurse

A farmer

A miner

A lorry driver

A dinner lady

ROB
A footballer

A police man

SUZY
An actress

BETHAN
A doctor

A milkman

A postman

An artist

A ballet dancer, and really soon.

A dentist

A barrister in court

The last child to call out is TOMOS.

TOMOS

The first man on the moon, an astronaut!

Acknowledgements

The Green Hollow was originally commissioned by BBC Cymru Wales and produced by BBC Studios Wales in association with VOX Pictures. I am especially grateful to Bethan Jones and Jenna Robbins for their support in the research and writing of the script, and to Pip Broughton and the cast for bringing it to the screen with such sensitivity and skill. None of this, however, would have been possible without the insights and generosity of those I interviewed as part of my research, and as such I would like to thank the following individuals and organisations: Janett Bickley, Jeff Edwards, Gaynor Madgwick, Gurraj Mann, Gurvinder Mann, Bernard Thomas, Mark Williams, Stephanie Davies, Professor Sir Mansel Aylward, Dave Evans, Gwyneth Evans, Sam Knight, Owen Money, Simone Roden and the children, teachers and parents of Ynysowen Primary School, Aberfan Community Library, Merthyr Central Library, Merthyr Leisure Trust, The Aberfan Wives Group, Trinity Childcare and Family Centre, Ynysowen Male Voice Choir. *Diolch o galon pawb.*